MYRTLE BEACH
BACK WHEN

The Grand Strand - Before The Beginning

A great white brow silently shifted sand.
Robbed of sixty million years of mellowing,
from Pliocene to Cretaceous flushed away,
no black earth held trees or rice -
a barren waste in times of wresting
bareboned life from land.

Along the sinewy rivers rice, timber, turpentine,
shipbuilding and deep water carried dreams
as far as Earth's corners. Life fleshed out.

A man came from the fullness on the rivers,
stood on the ocean brow.
He saw in the shifting sand
a place for vistas and visions,
for breathing and bathing.

On the rolling changing necklace of dunes
sea oats waved to gulls, bent to red-winged birds.
Yaupon and scrub oaks clustered high ground,
beach grass spread wiry in the low.
His wife saw glistening leaves on myrtle
clutching tawny sand,
cuddling the very crystal rim,
named it Myrtle Beach.

Visitors flocked to cool breeze,
semi-tropical nights,
the balm of a salty dip.

The red moon thrust a fresh washed eye
up and over, inspecting all changes.

Dedicated to
Franklin Gorham Burroughs

Several of these poems first appeared in
The Fayetteville Times, Saturday Literary Supplement
Fayetteville, North Carolina

MYRTLE BEACH BACK WHEN

ISBN: 0-932662-90-0

Printed for	St. Andrews Press
	St. Andrews Presbyterian College
	Laurinburg, North Carolina
by	Monument Printers and Lithographers, Inc.
	Verplanck, New York

| Cover Art by | Lou Quattlebaum |

| Book Design & Layout | Carol Tremblay |

| Scottish Logo | Ellen Walters |

MYRTLE BEACH BACK WHEN

Poems by Marie Gilbert

Sketches by Lou Quattlebaum

*Remembering long skirted days
is more than a wallow in nostalgia,
crystal from clear air rings to be heard.*

SCOTTISH
HERITAGE
SERIES

ST.
ANDREWS
PRESS

Contents

MYRTLE BEACH
BACK WHEN

Moving To The Cottage For The Summer

Whipped up in the dust of the chicken yard
Rhode Island Red feathers swirl,
hens flutter and sqawk as Kaleb
catches them one by one.
The brown paper bag folded up to half depth
that rides his close-cropped head
for such jobs as chicken chasing
and corn shucking, never wiggles
as he darts and dives for the plump hens,
smoothes their wings between his
two big hands, eases them in
eight little red hens in two crates fastened
to the bumper on the back of the Chrysler
for the ride to Myrtle Beach to spend the summer
laying eggs in the chicken yard bathed in ocean breeze
behind the cottage.

Moving down time is
June first, and day simmers early.

On the driver's side of the car
suitcases fit on the running board
behind the telescoping fence.
James removes his flat straw hat,
slips through to the driver's side.
Mattie sits beside him holding
fresh from the farmer's market
a coconut cake in a tin box balanced
on her lap, ready for the first
of the summer guests who'll arrive next day.
In the trunk of the car goes
the sewing machine, brown bags of groceries,
the peck measure, scratch feed for the hens.
In the back seat, Kaleb and the cook named Myrtle
flank a stack of brown paper packages -

sheets and towels to replenish last season's
wear and tear, and for the dining room and kitchen
newly made curtains to be hung
after all the windows are washed.

Rumble and roll forty miles an hour . . .
the road is paved 'most all the way.
Forty miles an hour wind form the tilted windshield
and from the side windows, stirs the heat
rising from the road to sit with them in the car.
From Florence, pass Gregg Camp and the Pee Dee,
Marion and the jail house on Freedom Corner,
Galivant's Ferry, Aynor, Cool Springs and Homewood
come to Conway. Rattle over the wooden bridges
curving and stretching on and on out of Conway,
come to Socastee.

                 And then-
begin to sit tall and watch for
a spread of blue at the end of the street
after the turn at Myrtle Beach Depot
after Chapins, Delta Drug, and the Sea Side Inn.
If the tide is high you'll get a glimpse
even of the spray and the surf
before turning left at the Pavilion
to lot #5, halfway to the Yacht Club
and the cottage on the right.

Getting there done, turn on the electricity,
the water. Take the feather pillows
down from the clothes line strung
for over winter in the back bedroom.
Make up the beds. Feed the hens
cackling and scratching on ground made new
by their winter absence. Put the rockers
on the porches in the breeze. By night
supper cooks on the big wood stove
and summer begins!

Sanctified Piano

In a struggle to keep keys from sticking
the upright Steinway draped in flowered flannel
under midnight velvet fringed green
hugs the rear of the run-through-hall
out of the salty breeze.
Alongside the hammers, a light bulb swings
leaking slant rays. The draping is lifted
to free the keyboard for little kids
playing *Chop Sticks* and *Mama, Mama Can You Tell,* for
big kids playing *Hall of the Mountain King*
la de da da da de da, hoping the keys won't stick,
for Cousin Fanny's fingers feeling out the chords
to *Ramona* and *Roses of Picardy,* for
Uncle Charlie plinking *Captain Jinks of the Horse Marines*
all week long -
but not on Sunday.

Before Cousin George comes down to visit,
Mr. Hoffman all the way from Florence
tunes that upright fine as salt air will permit
'cause those keys have to move, man move
all week long -
but not on Sunday.

On the radio, Georgie plays the latest
for the station up in Pennsylvania.

Wherever he plays, folks stop talking,
eyes widen, hips begin to twitch.
He plays *Sophisticated Lady* in ten fingered chords
that ooze down the keys close as cream,
he loves Gershwin and Hoagy Carmichael -
all week long -

On Sunday, he plays *What A Friend,*
Sweet Hour Of Prayer, In The Garden -

The Old Rugged Cross slips sideways
into syncopation,
his bass hand takes to bossing,
"Georgie!" Mama yells,
"Not on Sunday!"

Morning On The Back Porch

On the ocean side
the sun climbs blinding
steaming away night mists.
On the street side the house itself
makes long shadows across the chicken yard,
cool breeze wanders to the tune
of contented cackling, to the tune
of "clams, crabs" hawked from tubs, and
baskets brought to the back steps.

"Corn, butter beans, potatoes
squash, okra and tomatoes"
sings the driver to his mule
pulling the wagon slowly -
slowly enough for Kaleb in his brown bag hat
and Myrtle in her blue uniform dress
to step up to the swinging scales,
purchase from the driver.

The ice man, from the seat in his dray
reads the sign hanging on the porch post -
100 pounds or 50 pounds. His horse knows
just what to do. He waits while the ice man
hoists the heavy rectangles clamped in tongs
to melt and shine the black rubber on his back,
fits the new block into the box,
replaces the almost melted pieces on top
while children part the van's rear curtain,
choose pieces broken off in the sawing
to suck and hold in dripping fingers.
He waits while the ice man collects his coupons,
then he trots to the next house.

Big boys bring blackberries,
tales of thickets and rattlesnakes
to the back steps to sell to the tune
of a quart measure and jingling coins.

On the ocean side
the sun declares the weather.
Out back before the shadows shorten,
piles of butter bean hulls, corn shucks
and clam shells, stay cool and damp
to be read like the day's menu.

Hence, The Alarm Clock

Three little girls forget the heat of day sand.
With each hour that passes since sunset
the sand on the dune grows cooler-
soothes fingers slipping through.
Their nurse comes along
with an alarm clock set for nine p.m.

From the dune in the dark
they look to the light in the pavilion -
golden mellow the dance floor
golden mellow the music of fiddle and sax
trumpet and banjo that swings the ruffles
to follow the lead of starched linen trousers.
The nurse watches as she cushions the clock
carefully up out of the sand.

The moon smiles upon the dune where
slim frames in cool dresses dance within,
rehearse each dip, each smile
as limbs tense, relax in caressing sand.

So easy for eyes from the quiet dark
to grow heavy watching the golden sway.
The nurse, too, could be lost
in the delicious breeze,
slip of to sleep until some gull
calls to the sunrise.

More likely, parents would scurry through the night
scoop up with anxious arms
carry sand and all to waiting beds.

Morning Dip With Mama

"If you don't like washing your face before breakfast
come swim with me. That's the easy way to do it."

Her black wool suit a size for half again her height
hangs low and loose, - (She wants length for modesty?)
A red bath cap covers all but a few silver curls
peeping out at the nape of the neck.
Red bathing slippers bounce eagerly
on walks still night damp,
a cluster of grandchildren leave assorted footprints
behind her out to the sand. Calisthenics first.
Hands on hips, swing right, swing left.
Run in place, up, down, up, down.
They imitate her every move, glancing over shoulders
even at this early hour to be sure the beach
is theirs alone.

She leads the way knee-deep into the surf,
dips the right shoulder, the one that sometimes aches
dips the left shoulder, leaps over a wave,
submerges up to the chin in the calm deep that follows.

Splashing, chortling, all the while encouraging
her little entourage to join
the good fun she wants to share;
to pass along.

Chewing Gum Drawer

Papa's room is cool and dark,
varnished shutters cover four big windows
open to the deep porch.
Enter quietly on invitation to look up
to the chiffonier's top left hand drawer
holding the week's housekeeping money
mysterious as a vault. It smells of peppermint.
A small key he slips from his vest pocket,
the unfinished bottom of the drawer slides out,
the peppermint whiff grows stronger.
"P.K. Chiclets," he announces, "are made
with three separate packages inside!
Why?" His fingers divide the red lettered packs
of irresistable white, hand them down
to plump palms, "Because I had
three grandchildren born in one year!"

Perhaps Wrigley did
make P.K. gum for such a grandfather.

Breakfast At Eight

Bacon whiffs mingle with morning cool
speak as clearly as any bell or bugle -
nearly eight a.m.

Beside each place, orange juice fresh squeezed
set on blue checked damask, awaits arrivals,
blends with morning sunshine.

When all the chairs are filled
Mama reads the devotional,
and Papa asks the blessing.

Peaches, cantaloupe,
berries black or blue, the choice
depends on season and supply.

Subtle recognition comes for those
with hair still damp from swimming
earning semihero status.

Bacon and grits come with eggs poached,
soft boiled, fried, or scrambled,
toast, butter and apple jelly.

Charlotte Observer - State Paper
boys stagger the song as if on cue.
Money waits upon the porch ledge.

As if dessert belongs with breakfast,
pancakes come with boiled fruit syrup, or
Br'er Rabbit, or Log Cabin from the cabin can.

Linger over conversation and coffee, take the papers
to the porch to rock in the breeze, or
go play in the sand beneath the cottage.

Blam! Blam! Papa picks up his rocker by the arms
blams it down on the porch. Oh dear!
The boys left the wrong paper -
The raw deal paper - again!

On Stretching The Cottage

For an invitation
walk by Papa's office on a Tuesday.
He drives down to the cottage every Thursday.

"May I go to the beach with you?"
No listening for the answer,
just absorb the hug and the welcome.

Mama finds a space for any grandchild.
Accomodations, not the welcome, vary.
A front room with cousins is grand.

Share her bed if company fills the house.
Flat-a-back she barely uses half,
falls asleep quickly but, oh, so loudly!

To leave like a spoiled brat would flout
the take-us-as-we-are-and-always-welcome,
might even discomfort the visiting grownups.

She gentles a hand on each shoulder
any time you leave, with a quick kiss says
"Well, if you must, but come back soon."

Rain God Of The Land Beneath The Cottage

From the washbasin above, water
drains from the open end of a straight pipe,
rain from heaven, giving life to sand cities.

Water mixed with sand makes mortar
for shaping desert architecture
of homes, schools and public buildings,
for paving streets; water fills the
shell-lined canals that amble through
town and countryside to the very last
house on the irrigation system,
freshens the blue sandspur flowers and daisies
tucked into the landscape - water could,
if enough gentlemen shave in the morning.

Uncle Robert, more generous than Chac
the Mayan rain god awaiting a maiden thrown
into the cenote before saving life below,
washes and washes and washes -
waits - then suddenly pulls the plug
on a full basin of clear water

just to hear the children gasp,
stop rain dancing, start sandbagging.

He smiles benignly, as rain gods should,
chuckles in clean shaven fun.

15

Buried Watermelon

Back where the head room is low
under the kitchen end of the house
under the drip from the hole in the floor
beneath the icebox
the sand is always cool and damp.
Like as not a round spot of dark green
reveals a watermelon buried there
awaiting a slicing occasion.

Mealtime already an occasion,
never slice it then.
Not for breakfast, not for dessert
but midmorning, midafternoon, midnight,
after a swim, after fireworks, or
when company drops in.

With your fingers on the oil cloth
that covers the porch table, how far
can you flip a watermelon seed
quickly
when no one's looking.

World Travel

To the hand the wood feels smooth
and the eye begins to design.
Take short lengths carpenters toss aside,
position one atop another to create
vans, trucks, touring cars, sedans.
One nail will often do.

Soft and cool the sand on hands and feet.
Sun tanned arms and legs slide
stretch to tend life in sand cities
beneath the summer cottage,
drive cars through intersections
to the grocery, the post office and out
into vaste undulation of past footprints
scaped with wind from sea, out as far
as geography lessons feed imagination.

Cars glide up Mt. Mitchell, Pikes Peak
down into Grand Canyon,
run on fuel found in books to Taj Mahal
Zeider Zee, Serengeti, Matterhorn
streams are bridged, mountains tamed.
To chart a course comes easy in the sand.

Protected by the house above
and the life that moves within it,
covered as with umbrella -
ribs smooth and structured -
possibilities stretch
out to the end of yearning.

Visitors Beneath Our House

Coming up from a swim one Sunday morning
early glisten rests on a bundle under the porch -
two people rolled together in one blanket!
The beach is crowded on Saturday night.
Were rooms that hard to find? Costly, maybe.

Mama's concern shows more than she wants
and Papa, on his stiff leg, goes down to investigate.
There is conversation and then, "Mattie,
could you send two cups of coffee down?"
A young man and a girl soon walk away.

"They promised not to come again," Papa says.
"Don't play down there for a few days."
Mama instructs the assembled children.
Kaleb rakes the sand every day,
turning it, he says, to the sun and the fresh air.

Keeping Sunday
The Chapel On A Sandy Hill

Mama explained it over and over -
no way not to understand.

Coming to the beach for a week's vacation
is one thing. Coming for the day,
renting one of those black wool suits
white lettered Myrtle Beach Farms is another.

We were privileged to stay all summer
and at our house Sunday would be kept.

We would learn a Bible verse and
all the stanzas of one hymn,
we would attend Sunday School and Church.

Organdy so right in evening cool
scratches and prickles in morning's swelling heat.
Mary Jane pumps find every stubbed toe
every shell cut of the week's barefoot days.

Between Sunday School and Church
the two oldest grandsons ask permission
to sit with the Deacons on the back row.

"Rob and John are so grown-up,"
Mama beams as she walks down the aisle
to substitute at the piano.

The younger children snuggle in the pew with Papa
and any adults visiting the cottage,
vie to share his hymn book as they stand to sing
"I'm feasting on the manna."

Seated for the announcements, adults sway
funeral parlor fans, small hands wave bright
Sunday School papers, to delicately shoo the flies
and coax the breeze through screenless windows -

windows framing, between clumps of wind-smooth
myrtle dark green on yellow dunes, Rob and John
sauntering home.

This scene spreads before Mama
when she swings her four-eleven frame
'round on the piano bench
to put her feet on the floor.

Without hesitation
she sallies down the aisle.

During the Old Testament Lesson, all eyes
on one side of the church
watch through the row of windows.

She plows the loose sand
over the rolling dunes, a widgeon in full sail,
quickly catches two unsuspecting elbows.

The preacher almost finishes the New Testament Lesson
when back down the aisle they come, all three -
to the front row this time.

She unsnaps her beaded purse
hands them each a quarter
just before the plate is passed.

Mama sits at the piano bench
in time to play the Doxology.

The congregation stands
sings
with eyes straight ahead.

The Boardwalk

A sinew, the boardwalk stretches each year
from the Pavilion north and south
a tendon of weathered wood, rails the height
to perch upon in moonlight,
watch white rollers find the beach.

A level walk, its height above shifting sand
varies from five feet to resting on it.
Patching in spring keeps it free
of rotting wood. Cottages connect to it
in several ways, and some
have summer houses out on the dunes
creating a network of sociability
alive in moonlight.

Especially lively is the one
where the boy of the house, a genius,
wired the inviting seats of his gazebo.
Couples who rest when he is at the switch
sit briefly.

Just the width for couples to meet
and pass with ease, young men
use the boardwalk to collect their dates,
parade them in their long dresses
to the dance upstairs at the Pavilion
where grown-ups sit in rocking chairs
around the dance floor, reliving their youth.
Young children loll in their laps
watching and planning

except on Monday which is children's night -
when children march around the dance floor
under all those bright lights, sit upon it
to see the floor show of tap and acrobatic dancing,
march round again for favors of whistles or fans.
Some Monday nights are costume contests,
children parade as pirates, as majorettes
as ladies from Japan or Julius Caesar
for prizes of bright plaster statues.

Underneath the boardwalk, rain drops
through the cracks between boards
line the clean sand into neat perforations
as if for easy tearing.
A perfect place for hide-and-seek,
children run low between sand billows
as evening cools and grows dim.

One year, next to the Pavilion a merry-go-round
appears magically, as if grown over winter.
Calliope competes with the dance band upstairs.
Children race to parents for money to ride.

Papa leaves watching the dance
to sit on a boardwalk bench in the breeze
holding a roll of tickets.

Of all the circle of fairyland ponies
the palomino is the favorite. The white horse
is second - beautiful in leather bridle
jeweled with rubies and emeralds.
The black horse tosses his mane,
flairs his nostrils, seems dangerous.

Seasons flip from Labor Day to first of June.
Bingo in a tent, a ferris wheel, penny arcade,
an oriental gift shop spring up helter-skelter,
cluster on the boardwalk to give the sinew
a throbbing heart of frenzied beat.

One spring
a sterile strip of concrete
laid flat
dooms the shifting sand beneath
to stillness.
Railings, patched boards
ripped and hauled away
only the name
boardwalk
remains the same.

Uncle Charlie

When Uncle Charlie comes
bringing his wife Aunt Lula
they unpack and stay awhile.

He looks so much like Papa
no doubting they are brothers -
even to the way they dress -
stiff wing collar, straight tie in a bow
flat straw hat
grey suit weekdays, blue on Sunday.

They play setback alike - deal the cards
with aplomb knock on the table
teaming up to win no matter
how their wives scheme and giggle.

If he had eight grandchildren like Papa,
they, too, like Papa's,
would come to his defense when anyone teased.

But he didn't seem to sleep as much as Papa.

When the cottage sags with silence
after midday dinner
children slip out one by one
to whisper on the porch with Charlie.
When a quorum gathers, he makes his motion.
"I propose we walk to the Pavilion for cones."

Or, better yet is when he says,
"While you rested, I hid five nickels
right here on this porch. Wait!
No scrambling, tiptoe,
no falling over rocking chairs!
Walk quietly and look.

No squealing when you see one.
Don't tell a soul." He'd lean
his white head over and point
to one ear. "Just come tell me
where you see it. I'll keep score.
When everyone locates all the coins
we'll award the prizes."

Conspiratorial, it seems, to sneak about
peeking up, under, into,
poker-faced not to reveal what you find,
furtively watching the others
for giveaway glances.

Confederate grey trimmed white
the house provides a perfect place
for hiding nickels and now and then
a dime slipped into a crack
or held in place with chewing gum.

Before the summer of thirty-two
even through depression deepens
Papa thinks it wise to paint,
choses mustard yellow trimmed brown
perfect for hiding
the copper of pennies.

Distorted Saturday Afternoon

A new red bath cap over her Dutch bob,
well down over her ears
even the ocean seems muffled and far away.

The cap is level with the edge of her father's
black wool suit, half way to his knees
now it is wet. He arrived last night.
Already they have bounced
in and over the waves, Daddy more adventurous
than Mother and Aunts she swims with midweek.
She reaches up to clasp his always warm hand,
they walk to the pier and back, then

she sees what she can hardly believe -
a group of shells - two beautiful conches
a large angel wing, a giant cockle
and two moon shells all within a circle
drawn with a finger in the sand.

She begins to cradle them in her arms
too excited to notice the conversation
up in the tall air where her Daddy
talks to the man who has just rushed up.

Just as suddenly the two men
begin removing the shells from her arms
placing them in the hands
of a little girl about her size.

Sobs ooze from her chest.
The words, "My daughter drew a circle
about her shells before we went swimming."
never penetrates the muffled ocean
much less through the bath cap.

Sobs give birth to sobs.
Embarrassed, her Daddy pops
her wet suit bottom
causing cries of insult.

More embarrassed than ever
he snatches her off the beach,
one arm is all he holds,
her feet flutter to keep up
into the house
into the bathroom
and a spanking behind the closed door.

Reactions lead to reactions.
She locks the door when he leaves,
and wails and wails and wails.

When it is dark and the house is still
she creeps the little distance to her bed.
Suit dry now, salty sand between the sheets,
she snuffles to sleep, exhausted.

Morning brings sun and
"Ah, now you are a good girl."
She is too weary to decide.

All that day and the next
her cousins glance away
when she catches their eyes.

　　　　*****

As she grows taller, sees wider,
although nothing of value
survives the afternoon,
she does not remember the misery
so much as the warmth of a hand
and one of a string of varicolored days
woven into the fabric of a childhood.

The Fourth Of July

Trombone sun pops up, glistens the sea.
Today is the day for patriotism
independence and pride. Breakfast is downed,
unpacking begins of boxes of bunting stored
year after year for celebrating, decorating
on this day in July. On the porch, each banner
is shaken to wind that gobbles wrinkles.
Bights through grommets leave ends
for tying to banister.
Stripes in lengths of blue and red,
blue fields with stars and stars and stars,
hang secure. Over the door, Old Glory
flies according to rule.

Run down the steps out to the boardwalk,
see the grey cottage wrapped in a smile
of bunting bulging puffs breathing alive.

Look south and north, neighbors
drape banners to mark this day.

What a time for the camera!
Accordion bellows pulled out of the box,
in groups on the steps each one
is snapped at least twice.

At midafternoon, bring up from cool sand
under the icebox drip, watermelon
to slice with a flourish worthy
of Washington wielding his sword.

Supper's a picnic -
sliced tomatoes, fried chicken
potato salad, pickles and
lifted out of the wooden churn
that leaks and drips, a canister of ice cream
white as the stars on the flag.

When the bright sky turns to federal blue
way out on the sand where it is safe,
at the Pavilion big bronzed men
who lifeguard by day, scurry around in the dark,
put on a grand display of Roman candles
skyrockets shot over the sea
with a pop that means, "Look up!"
See a bright bud blossom with petals that shatter
shimmer, slip into night as the crowd gives
cheer after cheer after cheer.

And finally, the flag!
On a stand built for this night,
forty-eight stars flicker on brilliance of blue,
stripes blaze wavy as if in the wind.
Ooh! Then a hush falls over the crowd -
think of Washington, Jefferson
John Paul Jones, Sumter, Marion
and his men who gave us
this reason to stand up with pride
who gave us this something
to brighten and stiffen our lives.

The Mimic

Stuffed into the car we drive into the woods
leave the clean breeze of ocean front,
a sticky feel settles, with still air
understory hum of gnats and mosquitoes.

In a hard swept clearing
Miss Tilly's house hunkers on nubs of posts.
Chickens wander under, peck, gobble
any termite that rears its head.

Mama's hens lay their best
but sometimes Miss Tilly will sell a few eggs
if she has any to spare; and,
sometimes, moving like a reed she rises
from the swing, steps off the porch,
eases toward the car
her cotton skirt lapping her calves
like friendly puppies, and says
"I ain't got airy one."

Mama's youngest grandchild has wide violet eyes.
When she begins to walk, she tip toes,
when she begins to talk, she whispers.
Faintly, we hear as she tip toes about the cottage
"I ain't got airy one."
Around the porch, over and over to perfection
"I ain't got airy one."

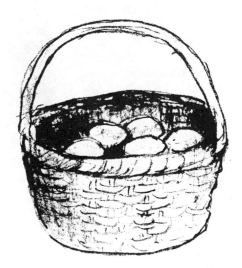

Servant Quarters

Myrtle sits on the low steps to her room
fanning with a rumpled paper
when supper is done. Red bandana replacing
the white cap of work day, her head
lolls on the door jamb,
soothing juice slips down from packed lip,
straw slides ease her feet.

Servant quarters attach to each garage
lining the street out back.

Behind the next cottage, another sits
wondering about home. From Conway, Columbia,
Chester, as far from Florence it seems
as Peru or Australia
shy reserve, even suspicion holds
but they begin to talk across the picket fence.
Away from home rhythms of hoeing gardens
hallooing neighbors, rocking on the porch at twilight,
they are friends, but slowly. Soon
they walk around to stroll the street together
or visit on the steps.

Out front the ocean murmurs cool,
breeze and low lights discourage mosquitoes.

Out back, the steps are used through sunset.
At dark, overhead lights turned to brightest
tight shades snug the August heat.

In the back bedroom of the cottage
where ocean speaks softly,
lie in bed listening.

Subtle as the yellow light
seeping through cracks,
libretto's precise edge blunted,
hear only round indigo tones ride
the rhythm of the night.

A Shell Of Motivation

Children of various sizes walk the beach.
Taller ones see a long way
move longer legs quickly to the best shells.

Small children, wool suits chaffing
between legs with every step
work by luck, trading for favors, or
largess from an older sibling
whose collection begins to overflow
allotted bench space on the back porch.

One girl has another trouble -
she can't learn to swim!
Calm water beckons beyond the waves,
she jumps, bucks waves, sputters face first.
Aunts, Uncles, cousins all try to help,
tell her she can do it, she flounders, sinks

until the day her brother holds up
a channel welk, a conche, she calls it,
a beauty, a perfect specimen
he has just found on the ocean floor.
"Swim over here," he calls, "and it is yours."

It glistens in clean wetness -
sun lit alabaster crown, rose inside -
as slowly he turns it in his hand.

She plunges forward, head up through spray,
slits for eyes she struggles
each breath half water.
Effort somehow eases to rhythm
a swimming stroke develops
her very own but it would do for now.

Her brother smiles,
"Now you know you can swim."

Costume Night

One evening friends blow in from the boardwalk
to visit Mama and Papa - keep coming
as if a storm were brewing until they fill
the long living room that runs through the cottage
with rocking and chatter and sliding of chairs
that edges the children away from the sofa and piano
into the bedroom to play.

Door closed, they jiggle on a bed
wishing it were the joggling board.
Ree grasps a blue kimono hanging on a wall peg
and twirls, bringing one fold up just beneath
her eyes. "Look!" Ginger squeals, "You're like
the picture on the Sunday School paper."
She reaches for the folder on the bedside table.
"See! Miriam at the well." She scurries
to the screened porch, returns
with an empty jug.
"I leaned the sea oats in the corner,"
she explains. "Balance this
on your shoulder with one hand.
The other hand can hold the drape
across your mouth - perfect!
You're Miriam."

Maxine opens the bedroom door.
Her most dramatic voice announces,
"Miriam going to the well." Ree saunters out,
weaves between rockers and outstretched feet.
Some adults look up and smile, some continue
talking. One lady reaches over to pat Mama
benignly on the hand, reaches the other way
to do the same for Papa. Aunt Betsy whispers
with emphasis, "You be careful of my kimono!"

Miriam returns from the well to find
Ginger buttoned snugly into little Jamie's
double-breasted jacket, red with brass buttons.
To the bureau mirror she practices stuffing
her tongue between her teeth and lips
twitching it monkey fashion.

She bounces on all threes, the fourth crooked up
to scratch here and there, improving
the performance at each roar from Ree and Maxie.
Swishing a hand towel off the rack, Maxie
folds a little monkey cap, fastens it
with bobby pins. Ginger bounces to the washbasin
grasps Papa's shaving mug to hold up between scratching.

For the organ grinder, Papa's coat will do,
his belt for a shoulder strap fastened
to a suitcase held level, waist high.
"Wait, you need a muffler." Ree runs back
to the boy's room for the plaid dresser scarf.

No announcement this time.
Out they pop into the crowd, Maxie humming
as loudly as she can, winding her hand at the side
of the suitcase as Ginger bounces among the guests,
head cocked, beguiling with her monkey antics
cruising the room and back.

The visitors depart soon -
maybe they would have anyway.

Creativity dried up, the girls count four nickels
in the mug. "Problem - that doesn't come out right
for three cones. How about one large chocolate soda
and three straws at Delta Drug tomorrow?"
To Maxie's question, "Yea! Yea!
but no fair blowing through the straws!"

Being Sent Home On The Bus

The threat is real!
Who wants to leave the ocean
and cousins playing in the sand.

Who wants parents waiting at the station
after reading a telegram saying
you've been sent home on the bus,
disobedience is not tolerated.

Eight grandchildren struggle
to live by house rules.
'Long about sixteen
problems begin to mount.

Ten-thirty is the hour -
all must be in by then.

At the Myrtle Beach Pavilion, intermission
is at ten-thirty! The dance goes on 'til one.
"To be in at ten-thirty is out of the ark!"
sobs Rob to John, "What do we do?"
They are the oldest, hit the impasse first.

Because the threat is real
they come in at ten-thirty,
slam the door and lock it for the night,
waking the household, especially Mama who
comes to kiss them goodnight
inhaling quickly, accurate as a revenooer
checking for signs of tobacco and alcohol.

Pleased and proud she is to see
them go to their room, listen
contentedly from her bed
as they drop shoes upon the floor
waiting for her to drift off to sleep.

Their windows open to the porch.
The screens unhooked for easy exit
wave quietly, awaiting their return
after the dance is over.

Woe is the moonlit night that finds her
rocking on the porch enjoying the ocean breeze
watching, waiting.

"Leave on the eight-fifteen bus!"
is all she says.

At quarter to eight she comes
with a tumbler of orange juice fresh squeezed
for each. She sits on the edge of the bed
to talk things over.

On her horizon
hope always hangs
full and ripe.

Real as knowing you've caused distress
the threat is a clanging buoy
riding the mainstream
tempering sallies into unknown waters.

Hot Footing

To walk black pavement in bare feet -
asphalt that's hotter than
boards or white concrete -

take a Dixie Cup of cracked ice,
drop a piece and step, drop and step.
You'll find the pavement pretty nice.

When Nor'Easters Blow

Even in summer, nor'easters blow now and then -
scouts sent in for three days
by restless winter storms
impatient for their time.
Froth whips to dirty foam as frenzied ocean
house cleans - sudden spits of rain
pelt from scuttling clouds.

A time for long sleeved shirts, and
when Michigan poker ceases to be fun,
story telling, trooping down to see
Miss Margy, dean of tales from back when.
Her house is shingle stained pine green,
the roof slants from a high point to low eaves
protecting her porch from sun and rain.
Lattice with cucumber vines filters west sun
making a cool cave for pine green rockers,
even the nor'easter seems far away

as her high top black shoes, she wears
out of habit. "Would you believe"
and she is off telling of the train,
"The Black Maria was the grand way to come
to Myrtle Beach even if sparks did shower
the passengers in open coaches.
Yes, black all over, long sleeves, high neck
was the best dress for travel.
When emergencies arose, such as sick children,
someone fired up the engine and raced twenty miles
to fetch the doctor, it was wise to be ready."
Oh the drama she could cast.

"Cattle, hogs and goats - goats"
She loves to tell about the goats.
"Wandered those dunes out there
where the bingo tent is, eating every blade.
At the hotel over there," she gestures
south to the Seaside Inn, "The cook
could never have managed without the goats.

The fishermen went out when the weather was right,
the two wheel cart came with fresh beef
covered with myrtle branches
to keep off flies, but then
there wasn't any ice to hold food over.
The chickens about were mostly for eggs.
When the sea was too rough, and
the wagon road rained out,
those goats were just there, on the hoof
waiting to fill in. The cook complained
he had cooked goat every way he knew,
the hotel guests had consumed so much goat
they were beginning to walk the banisters!"

She loves our laughter and hurries on.
"The name Myrtle Beach was chosen by vote
at the old Pavilion one night.
Edgewater was the runner up.
With all the myrtle bushes about
I like Myrtle Beach better, don't you?
We didn't used to think being so close
to the ocean was the best choice.
Now your Grandfather built as close as allowed.
I bet you think I have a "third row" cottage
but I like it here, and this spot used to be
as close as anyone wanted to be
to that big ocean.
The bath house was down there.
The shower was a barrel overhead. Water,
maybe sun warmed, maybe not
funneled through ice pick holes in a tomato can."

Encouraged by our glee, she tells
of the daring boys and girls who wanted
to swim on Sunday when the train didn't run.
The young men pumped the hand car all the way
pulling back and forth like rowing a boat.

"Did you come?"

"No-o-o, that was daring and scandalous."

"But earlier than that, I went camping
at what you call Singleton Swash,
up on the high place under the scrub oaks.
Oh! It was beautiful. For tents and provisions,
we had wagons brought part way
by river from Conway. We'd run along side,
we could ride but we never did.
My mama had a buggy. Once it stuck in sand,
men on horseback had to lift it out,
nearly tipped it over.
To cross the swash we'd arrive at low tide
so the wagons, buggy, those on horseback
and those on foot could cross
to the heavenly breeze, the clams and crabs
begging to be gathered. You will never know
how grand it was." She looks away
reviewing the scene.

Clams - makes us think of fritters.
The clam man came this morning.
We say our good-byes, walk home
while the rain is slacked,
spank bare feet in puddles on wooden walks.

For a short time, nor'easters aren't all bad.

Eunice, Where Is Eunice

Something between a shout and a song
jolts the world from dense sleep of early night
into black that fades grey around porch lights
and that all revealing moon shining
on the castaway weaving down the boardwalk.

Bump the rail right, bump the rail left -
slow forward progress - "Eunice, Eunice"
he sings in woe that strikes terror
to hearts flat in beds pushed up to double windows
open wide to porches.

Bump the rail right, then left
then right down our walk -
two feet wide, three feet above sandspurs
and no rail. Weave over to one edge
weave over to the other edge all the way
to our steps and up. "Eunice, Eunice!"
he wails as he shakes our fastened screen door.

Children lie frozen in fear.
Papa in Florence, Mama alone
unless the older boys have slipped
back in the porch window.

Again the screen rattles and strains the latch.
Rob goes to the door and says,
"Eunice doesn't live here."
Thank goodness he's home.
"Where is she? She won't let me in."
"House party people" Mama cntones
"Poor man." Even in the dark you know
she would grab a white ribbon for WCTU
and pin it on him if she could.

"Eunice isn't here?
Turn on your porch light
so I can see your steps."

Salt air has corroded the porch light.
Even the bulb is gone. A loud click
resounds as John flips the switch.

"Thank you, thank you. I can see
just fine now." He steps down the stairs
placing his feet precisely
and turns toward the pavilion.

The house drops back into silence
of God fearing folks - for the moment.

At the next walk, he turns in.
Quietly now up to the steps, the porch,
through the window - the screen is old and weak -
and into the bed beside it he collapses.

Mrs. Cohoun, the lady sleeping in the bed,
is also old and weak but she can scream,
Oh how she can scream.
She vacations with her husband
who benefits from sun and salt air.
He wags his cane and helps her yell.

Rob and John pull pants on over their pajamas,
no time to go around the walk,
dash across the sandspurs.
They walk the sleeping drunk out
and down the boardwalk to a bench
in the shelter of the Pavilion.
Covered with Mrs. Cohoun's blanket -
she'd never care to see that blanket again -
they leave him to sleep
and to wait for Eunice.

After breakfast the next day, the Cohouns leave,
Rob and John put suitcases
into the car for them.

Days pass,
Mama chooses to let the lesson
speak for itself.

When Margaret Visits

Cousin Margaret from Pennsylvania comes to visit
every summer, shaking out chiffons, spreading them
to toss their wrinkles in the breeze.
Her lively eyes are round and dark,
large enough for one to fall into headfirst.
With pink clips she wears when she retires
she crimps narrow waves into brown hair
lightly graying, braids it back with a fillip
and tortoise pins.

Watching her daughter stroll
with her fiance' on the boardwalk,
she smiles. "Young love is so very tender."
But when she greets her George who comes
for the last few days of her yearly visit,
older love seems neither stale nor calloused.

One summer she comes as a widow.
Her soulful eyes brim now and then.
She slips into the bedroom to empty them
like cups too full. Dear Margaret,
dear, dear Margaret, Mama worries.

A handsome judge, a widower, comes to visit
in the cottage next door - a cottage near enough
for exchange of pleasantries during the day's
comings and goings affording ample opportunity
for proper introductions.

One evening, the Judge calls on Margaret.
She receives him out on the porch.

Close behind shutters on the windows to the porch
children lie flat abed, eyes stretched, listening,
hoping to learn of courtship and the language of romance,
hear rock, rock of chairs, light laughter, ocean cooing
hear voices, but no words
as south southeast breeze blesses
the moonless night.

Next morning at breakfast
she seems a little brighter.

Tall Uncles In The Surf

When the tide is high
and the beach is narrow,
when beyond the breakers is deep water,
it takes a lot of tall uncles
to keep a girl afloat - dog paddling
from one to the other
touching the wool suit strap buttons
bouys on the top of strong shoulders.

It only takes a touch
for confidence.

Learning About Sewing

Since the machine is at the beach
how nice, I thought, to learn to sew
between swims and other fun. Mama
will teach me, pleased I want to know.

I choose a pattern and some cloth.
Mother buys them in good faith.
I stroke the blue print eager to start
never wanting to wait.

Aunt Ginger says, "Find the guide,
I think the pattern is pretty."
She shows me how to pin it
as she spreads the cloth expertly.

Aunt Lula who had been a nurse
comes with scissors sharp.
"Let me show you how to cut it
then you'll be ready to start."

Mama comes to demonstrate
how to pin and baste.
To stitch upon the sewing machine
peddle with care, never in haste.

Aunt Betsy says, "Only facing
and the hem left for you!
You could wear this dress tonight!
Your summer project's through."

Learning About Crocheting

Perhaps I could crochet
enough to piece a runner.

A frail maiden lady comes to visit Mama
offers to teach me how.

Her instructions are explicit
when we sit down to start.
Her bony fingers, stiff
crochet with frightening vengeance,
I try to imitate, find plump fingers
won't crook no matter how I twist them.
She tugs and jerks along,
I turn to nerves and knots.
No way I'll ever learn.

At sight of a crochet hook
my fingers start to fight
feel stiff and crooked.

Learning About Knitting

Aunt Betsy sits and rocks
on the porch in the breeze,
the chair beside her open
for a child wanting to talk.
She listens, smiles and listens,
comments now and then.
All the while I watch her fingers
knitting boucle' dresses
she'll wear for church or tea.
Her fingers move with grace and rhythm
even though they fly
they never seem to hurry
agitate or tire.
I watch until one day I blurt out,
"Aunt Betsy, could you teach me that?"
She answers, "Why of course,
it's fun, you could learn."

She finds some nice-sized needles
for small hands to hold,
snow white yarn
pretty and easy to see.

It's grand to hear the rhythmical click,
to watch my knitting grow,
to feel the slip of yarn pass along
and along and along.

The Fishing Boat Goes Out

Eight fishermen come silently
working to mellow command
to muscle the weathered boat part way on logs
drag it over the sand
leaving keel track into the sea.
Thick gunwales notched from the saw of drop lines,
scarred from big fish caught and sharks cut loose,
they grasp to wade beside the boat
up to their thighs, steady it into the waves.
With a quick vault to seat, back to the sea,
they row through the breakers and beyond.
Rhythm flows a chain from oar to oar
from shoulder to shoulder.
Forearms gleam strong black
in early glisten.
Men and boat become
a speck in dawn's pink
and disappear.

The cry moves from cottage to cottage,
the fishermen are out!
Housewives plan for fish by noon.

Through the morning, swimmers watch
wonder if the fishermen found the rock reef
hidden fifty feet below,
the place where fish come hungry.
And then -
the speck reappears
grows larger on blue sky.

Some off porches, out of houses
some in wet swim suits come out of the water,
folks stroll along the strand guessing
where the boat will beach,
run forward when it shoots the breakers.

Give the money to the cook.
She knows just what she wants.
Blue uniform dresses, white aprons
with wide straps, barefeet enjoying
the excuse to wade, rush to the fishermen
who jump out holding strings of bass, trout
black fish, make quick deals
even as they beach the boat.

On the hard sand fishermen toss
skate, sting ray, blowfish
and shark, as if to amuse.

The crowd disperses. In low silence
eight men heave the ponderous craft back
up to the dunes, carry their oars home.

Who owns the boat is not a question.
Through weight alone it belongs
to those with skill and strength.
Even thieving ocean only swamps it now and then
leaving it filled with sand - high on the strand
for little folks to climb into and over
playing Coast Guard and pirate; it weathers
awaiting another day, another trip when
men and boat merge to slip over the water
out of the sight of land's world
out to the rocks for fish.

Ritual Of The Afternoon Dip

When the punishing sun weakens about four o'clock
they come down to the sea in black and midnight blue
suits of wool, less scratchy when wet
but soggy - stretching from round neck and shoulder straps
to halfway between thigh and knee
and for ladies, a doubleness of skirt over pants -
no stockings for these ladies, only bathing slippers
red or blue trimmed in white and matching caps
riding low on foreheads, snuggling ear lobes.

Daring men swim out beyond the pier,
elbows high out of the water. Ladies
dip one shoulder at a time into the froth
of rolling waves, hold hands and jump
with little children whose suits are made like theirs
with red stripes or orange. Girls wear matching caps
but some wear no bathing slippers
risking cuts from shells
bites from crabs. In sandy puddles
they sit and soak, making drip castles.
The breeze caresses them.

When the cottage roof shadows crawl over the dunes,
two at a time they leave, sandy wool chafing
with every step, to walk the raised wooden way
around the cottage to a pair of showers
on the back porch. Myrtle and Kaleb wait
with tubs of fresh water, cotton robes
in several sizes, towels and clothespins.

Step into the tub at the foot of the steps
to wash off the feet, up the steps
to the shower. Unbutton the straps and let
the soggy heaviness drop. Crack the shower door,
pitch the bath suit out - splat - on the porch floor.
Myrtle will wash it in a tub of clean water,
Kaleb will ring and twist it shapeless
pin it by the shoulder straps to drip
on the line under the porch eaves.

The shower is cool and clean.

Towel off, put on your robe from the peg.
Carrying the cap and slippers you rinsed and dried
parade across the porch and down the hall
to your room. Feel clean and refreshed.

Now's the time for chiffon, high heeled slippers,
dusting powder and upswept hair for ladies;
for little girls, organdy with picoted ruffles,
wide ribbon sashes, silk socks, Mary Jane pumps
and Johnson's powder on skin sun pink.

Supper will be shrimp and clam fritters,
potato salad and sliced tomatoes
and caramel cake.

The afternoon nap assures
you're fresh for evening fun.
Walk the boardwalk north to the Yacht Club
where live music floats from the dining room,
cards are played in the lobby.
Walk out on the pier to see what fish were caught,
brace against the wind and watch
the lights dance zig-zag in the ocean, or
walk south to the Pavilion to rock
in high back chairs, watch the beautiful dancers
wheel 'round the shining floor.

One Way To Learn To Dance

La da ' da, la da ' da *Sunrise Serenade*
Glenn Miller, Benny Goodman, Tommy Dorsey,
*Moonlight Serenade, I'm Getting
Sentimental Over You* - What a summer
to find a handsome cousin
eight years older and so glamorous
wanting to show you the latest
in dancing. Heaven!

Any nickelodeon under the Pavilion
or at the Delta Drug soda fountain has
a spot for dancing barefoot. Shag -
done close with a guiding hand
between the shoulder blades
saying just what the girl should do -
all that yankee dancing he showed me.
"From my hand and your shoulder blades down
be limp like an old dishrag," he'd say.
We fed nickels to the juke box
to call up big band sounds, *Deep Purple,
Stairway To The Stars*, and practiced every chance.

Late in the summer, at the Pavilion
upstairs where the live band plays
upstairs with all those smooth dancers
on the shiny floor under all those lights
he took me out to dance with him -
a girl break early in the week -
scared. So scared I kept thinking
of the wet dishrag
so if I tripped over my feet
I'd trip to the heavenly music,
glued to the hand between my shoulder blades.

By the time my cousin came home from Princeton
at Christmas, I'd learned
for dance instruction for me
Mama paid him by the hour -
twenty-five cents an hour
I think they said.

The Ladies Aid Society Visits Mattie

Here they come -
sixteen ladies in three cars at ten a.m.!
They must have left Florence on the dot of seven.

Careful on the walk one board wide
over sand and sand spurs
down to the cottage they bring satchels

of bath suits, bath caps and slippers,
hat boxes of cakes and surprises
enough for twenty or more!

Mattie has been up since six,
skipped her morning swim to make potato salad
iced tea and lemonade for twenty or more

while Myrtle fried chicken
made biscuits and cobblers
for twenty or more.

When Mattie sits at the upright Steinway,
plays *Brighten The Corner Where You Are*
the meeting jollies to order.

Ever since the cottage was built, this summer ritual
rolled 'round second Wednesday in June
like full moon tide in marsh grass.

The Ladies Aid Society survived hard times
war, epidemic and the Presbyterian turn
to circles of ladies rotating every year.

For those who go bathing, grandchildren
emerge from play beneath the house,
take seriously their assignment

to give a hand on the tricky steps to the beach -
"You have Mattie's brown eyes"
"You're thoughtful like your Uncle Robert."

Lunch, peace, plenty
and for this day
troubles lie at rest.

To children playing in the sand beneath,
the program upstairs after lunch is a mumble
punctuated with laughter, with singing,

up to the silence that holds the Mizpah
followed by all verses of *'Til We Meet Again*
sung slowly as if the end should never come.

Chairs scrape the floor
ladies rustle up belongings
settle again into the cars.

Grandchildren cluster about Mattie
wave vigorously as she had instructed
hardly hearing her murmur

"This is the last time they'll come"
as she gazes after them. Clouds of dust
lift, brighten the setting of the sun.

The Fire

The acrid smell comes first -
during the suppertime lull
near the corner across from the Pavilion
through the roof of a cottage
flames break.
Sounds quickly surge cacophony -
fire trucks, hoses, commands shouted.
The curious run south,
the frantic run north.

Summer had been winding down.
Mother and I were staying over
so Rob could finish out his summer job
at the Pavilion for Speedy Spears.

A strong wind blows from the south.
A second house
flames.
The street between our ocean front
and the second row is not wide. Quickly
it fills with people and equipement.
Mother decides, "Take the car
out of the garage before the road is blocked,
move it to a safer place.
We may need it before this night is over."

Rob comes up on the run.
"Speedy sent all his help to the Pavilion roof
to put out sparks. From there I saw our roof
and knew I should come home!" He dashes
to the garage for the ladder,
Mother backs the car out smack
into the stream of traffic.
Rob puts the ladder up to the roof
at the low place over the back door.

The south wind whips red tongues
up into the night, lifts
burning hunks the size of tennis balls
to land on our roof that offers
wood shingles sun crisp. Flames
move north to lick the third house.

Carrying a bucket-a-water, Rob courses
the roof dousing burning debris.
I climb the ladder with a full bucket,
return with the empty one.

Fire trucks move north, nearer us,
concentrate water power
on the Blue Sea Inn. An alley
separates it from the three-storied inn
crackling to the south.

I muscle a full bucket
to the roof, see the ocean
crimson.
Neighbors bathed in eerie light stand
on the boardwalk in little groups
with furniture moved out of their cottages,
bureau mirrors glow red.

Burning hunks curve higher
land faster. Rob races over the roof peak
and down dousing here, there
faster than I fill the bucket,
hoist it up the ladder.
Only two buckets and a washtub -
what to do, what to do!
Across the street houses line up -
matchboxes waiting to spark and crumble.

Now
do the sparks begin to diminish?
Yes. In the alley
by the Blue Sea Inn
the firemen have held!

Rob comes down, we sit on the walk
exhausted and dirty,
notice the wind has changed.
It's blowing from the north!

After walking through the streets
teeming with people and traffic, Mother
returns; says she hopes tomorrow
she can find where she left the car.

"What is the washtub doing on the roof?"
she asks. It is a wide tub
with handles on two sides.

Wearily Rob climbs the ladder.
"It's full of water," he reports,
and then to me, "You must have brought it up -
walked up this ladder
as if it were a set of stairs."

The three of us move around the porch, see
the blood-red ocean fade to night blue,
see the neighbors move their furniture
back into their cottages,
stand a moment
acknowledging
the cool north wind.

Papa On The Porch - A Soliloquy

The little fellow thought I was asleep.
Perhaps I was dreaming, day dreaming
sliding in and out, it's hard to tell these days.

He'll come again, watch me a moment
from under sandy bangs, then slip away.
He looks so like Mattie, and he's sturdy
like her father.

                    Her father, now
he was a Scot to reckon with,
wouldn't let me have his daughter 'til
he felt I could provide for her!
I guess he was the goad
that made my store a quick success
made me save by sleeping on a cot
in the storeroom, made me learn about
the thread and linen those ladies in Florence
wanted for their fancy work.
I had to bring the best from Philadelphia
to please them.

How those train whistles blew! I can still feel
the bustle, hustle of passengers coming in
to the growing town.

I managed to build a hotel.

With two hands on his knee, he shifts
his stiff leg on the banister that
braces him back in the rocker.

That's when he let me wed her!
He couldn't know how hard she'd work -
just as hard as I did - up at dawn
running the dining room. Drummers,
circuit judges, tobacco buyers and auctioneers
all the regular travelers stopped with us
because of her more than because of me.
I couldn't have done without her!

It's hard even now
after three and a half years.

I have to last 'til fall when I'll be eighty,
she made it to eighty. She just lay down and died
after packing clothes for Thornwell Orphanage
all day long, boxes to the parlor ceiling.
Her way was better.

South southeast from the sea
the breeze stirs short wisps of hair.
His neat white head rolls sideways
on the high back of the rocking chair.
Under glazed eyes and heavy lids
he drifts on.

We had a nice apartment at the Hotel
on the second floor - room enough for all four
children and for us, sunny big windows to the floor.
Those windows - how many times
I've thought it through, fought it through
trying to rewrite it.
It remains the same.
I called our youngest who was three,
"Come, Matt, come. Come here to see the parade!"
He came, but not to me.
He ran to the other window.
It was open.
There was a gasp from the crowds
in the street below.

I cry even now.
Mattie grieved until she broke,
and broke again and still
she worried about my grieving.

People say time heals sorrow.
It only appears that way.
Things are never the same again.

A house - the other three were growing up,
perhaps the time had come to build a house -
a big one - being accustomed to a hotel
it would have to be a big one.
We laughed at ourselves later.
We built three houses,
each larger than the other,
but never got that feel we'd grown to know
living in a hotel.

Planning a house seemed to brighten Mattie.
She wanted brick, a round room and a tower.
Lying in bed one night she told me
just how she thought it ought to be.
"We'll have young ladies bustled and parasoled
slender as willows, promenading on a blue green lawn
clipped, bordered with sweet william.
They'll point dainty slippers out from layers
and layers of ruffled embroidery
white on cool white. They'll smile, nodding pompadours
on swanlike necks to young men in grey waistcoats
who offer the strength of an elbow
to support one dainty kid gloved hand,
as they stroll in pairs to a seat in the cool shade
of the latticed summer house dripping wisteria."

She laughed when I told her
she painted quite a sugary scene.
I guess it was
like that now and then.

Adjusting suspenders over his thin-striped shirt
he stretches, shifting in the rocking chair.

Now this beach house we built plain
but we used good lumber
built it strong as one in town.
We planned this porch just right.
Three sides around the house it goes,
but here on the south corner, all the rockers
seem to cluster near the hammock.

We did a good thing building this house.
The eight grandchildren still seem to enjoy it.
If I stop a second, I hear
mixed with surf murmur a sea gull cry
that sounds like squeals coming from under the porch
where grandchildren played in the tawny sand
when they were little, planned shows
in the piano box.

That was Mattie's idea.
When the piano came by train from Florence,
out on the dray to our house, I would have
chopped up the box it came in for firewood,
we need it, sometimes in June, but
Mattie said we should have the men
open it carefully, put the box upright
in the sand beneath the house, with the side laid
flat for a porch. She used green paint to outline
a window in the rear and hung a curtain.
The play house became a theatre,
so she found some benches for the audience.
The little girls sang *Shuffle Off To Buffalo*
and danced a little jig.
Wearing their kimonos, they'd have an oriental
drama, tug the curtains, pretend to
peer out the painted window,
declare they saw someone coming.

I almost feel half a dozen soft hands
over my hands
with their eager invitation to come,
the show is ready to begin,
the admission is ten cents each --
meaning ten cents for each of them.

Those summers I went to Florence
every Monday morning, attended to business,
returned on Thursday after Kiwanis.
The road improved as years went by
making the trip shorter. I couldn't
have done it as long as I did
if it hadn't.

              Mattie and I had some good times!
Those setback games with Charlie and Lula!
We'd keep a running score for weeks.
Brothers sort of read each other's minds,
I guess. Charlie and I nearly always beat 'em.

He glances at a thin gold watch he slips
from its pocket, pries himself up
by the rocker arms.

Daughter and all the house guests
will be up from naps and heading
past me to the beach for a swim.

He steadies himself on his cane
strokes his chin.

I shaved this morning, didn't I?
I better go button a collar on my neckband
and find my string tie.

Marie Gilbert, a native of Florence, South Carolina, is a graduate of Rollins College. She and her husband live in Greensboro, North Carolina and spend a great deal of time at DeBordieu Colony in Georgetown, South Carolina. They have a son, a daughter and four granddaughters.

Other books by the author:

From Comfort *(1981)*

"Hers is a yearning to probe deeply and snatch moments of revelation . . ."

- - James Rogers
Editor Emeritus, Florence Morning News

+

The Song and The Seed *(1983)*
-with sketches by Lou Quattlebaum

"The poems are strong on emotion, rich in local color and good with dialogue."

- - Roy Parker
Editor, The Fayetteville Times

+

Forever New
-with art by Lou Quattlebaum

"There's always a sense of discovery, a sense of wonder, in the poetry of Marie Gilbert . . . "

- - Sam Ragan
Editor, The Pilot, Poet Laureate of N.C.

Lou Quattlebaum, a native of Cheraw, South Carolina, granddaughter of F.G. Burroughs (founder of Myrtle Beach) lives at Arundel Plantation near Georgetown. She is a Fine Arts graduate of William and Mary College. Her paintings and batiks are in many private collections and have been exhibited in major state galleries.

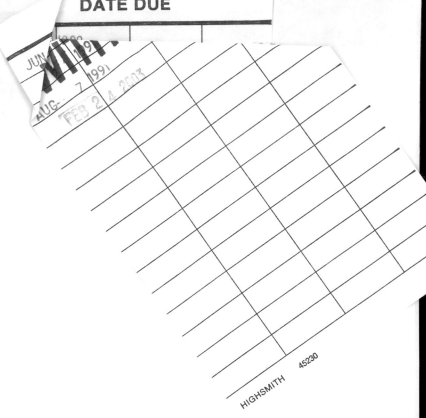